1 5

Puzzle Power

Puzzle Power

How to Jump-Start
Your Mind

Terry H.
Stickels

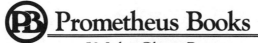
Prometheus Books

59 John Glenn Drive
Amherst, New York 14228-2197

Published 2004 by Prometheus Books

Inquiries should be addressed to
Prometheus Books
59 John Glenn Drive
Amherst, New York 14228–2197
VOICE: 716–691–0133, ext. 207
FAX: 716–564–2711
WWW.PROMETHEUSBOOKS.COM

08 07 06 05 04   5 4 3 2 1

Library of Congress Cataloging-in-Publication Data

Stickels, Terry H.
    Puzzle power : how to jump-start your mind / Terry H. Stickels.
        p. cm.
    ISBN 1–59102–203–7 (pbk. : alk. paper)
    1. Puzzles. I. Title.

GV1493.S834 2004
793.73—dc22

2004050351

Printed in the United States of America on acid-free paper

Contents

Introduction

The most important tool we possess in differentiating us from our peers and competitors is our ability to think. The way we express those thoughts says volumes about us from the first sentence. Not only are you judged immediately by the way you communicate, people inevitably start drawing conclusions about your thinking level. It stands to reason then that the better our thinking skills, the better we stand to be successful. This naturally prompts the question, "Is there anything I can do to increase or enhance my thinking skills and mental flexibility?"

The answer is yes. Recent findings in the field of neuroscience and cognition conclusively show that new, more powerful brain connections can be created with "mind-stretching" activities. And what might those be? Interestingly, some of the strongest evidence finds games and puzzles at the top of the list.

One of the best examples of this lies in Minnesota with the nuns of Mankato, many of whom are now in their eighties and nineties. These remarkable women, featured in *Time* magazine in 2001, are energetic, bright, and in excellent physical condition. They follow a rigorous routine of both mental and physical exercise. Two of their favorite activities they credit for their mental acuity are games and puzzles. Not only have they slowed down the aging process, but they keep adding to their mental acumen and flexibility.

The ongoing research in the cognition field by notable scientists such as Drs. Denise Park, Fred Gage, Jeffrey Macklis, and John Ratey points clearly to actively exercising your brain in much the same manner we work out physically: fun challenges from different approaches.

"Brain cells actually thicken when you solve puzzles and play games."
Gene Cohen
Former Director National Institute of
Mental Health Center on Aging

The idea of solving puzzles to increase your mental abilities is not a new concept. It is also an idea that has been taken seriously by some heavyweight thinkers. For example, Charles Sanders Peirce, considered by many to be one of America's great philosophers and mathematicians, was convinced that the methods used in schools to teach subjects that required thinking skills resulted in holding back good thinkers and actually identified some bright children as poor students. His solution was to introduce puzzles into the curriculum. He filled three notebooks with novel ways of using puzzles, games, and toys to introduce various concepts. He often asked teachers to let him instruct a group of youngsters who detested mathematics and seemed incapable of learning it. In one case, two of those students led their school as the best mathematicians—and this after a mere ten lessons. Well-known physicist and Nobel laureate Richard Feynman was one of the biggest advocates of puzzle solving as a means to becoming a better thinker. Not only was he an avid puzzle solver himself—he was quoted as saying, "I will spend an infinite amount of time on a puzzle," but he once proposed an entire curriculum composed of puzzles and games to the California Board of Education. He was thoroughly convinced that his methods would produce much better critical thinkers than the conventional curriculum.

"In a recent study it was found that adults with hobbies that exercise their brains—such as reading, puzzles, games such as chess—are 2.5 times less likely to have Alzheimer's disease."

Dr. Robert P. Friedland
Associate Professor Neurology,
Case Western Reserve University,
School of Medicine

Dr. John Ratey's book *A User's Guide to the Brain* offers compelling evidence as to the efficacy of using puzzles and games to boost mental flexibility. He writes, "Activities that challenge your brain actually expand the number and strength of neural connections devoted to the skill." He goes on to say, "We always have the ability to remodel our brains. To change the wiring in one skill, you must engage in some activity that is unfamiliar, novel to you but related to that skill, because simply repeating the same activity only maintains already established connections. To bolster his creative circuitry, Albert Einstein played the violin. Winston Churchill painted landscapes. You can try puzzles to strengthen connections involved with spatial skills. . . ."

Progressive companies are now recognizing the benefits of a workforce of critical and creative thinkers. Author and lecturer Michael Michalko's best-selling book, *Thinkertoys*, has been labeled "the business book of the nineties." What sets it apart from other business books? It is the use of Michalko's Thinkertoys—activities in puzzle formats that steer the brain into discovering new ideas, offering approaches to decision making and increasing one's creativity.

Such corporations as AT&T, Arthur Andersen, IBM, United Airlines, Chevron, Intel, and Liberty Mutual now hold problem-solving sessions utilizing puzzles of all varieties: logic, spatial/visual, word puzzles, and board games. These companies realize the importance of the skills and tools these puzzles bring by engaging participants in rigorous, thought-provoking activities.

More than ever, America's corporations are demanding better critical and creative thinkers. Having impressive degrees from prestigious universities is not the main prerequisite for success as it once was. Thinking skills are. Winston Churchill was on the money with his famous quote "All the great empires of the future will be empires of the mind."

Puzzle solving leads to the development of skills that give you the competitive advantage you need outside the walls of your company—and inside your offices as well. In business, you are not only constantly challenged to beat the companies that are your daily competition, but you are also required to fight for your own survival among your coworkers. You need every tool you can lay your hands on to win both wars.

The puzzles in this book were designed to challenge you—and they are fun to solve as well. Be creative in your puzzle-solving efforts. Look at these as more of a game than a task. This is the way great thinkers approach problems across the thinking spectrum. They see most mental confrontations as games or puzzles and set no limits to find their solutions.

Along the way, I'll help you with solving tips and introduce you to some universal characteristics of great thinkers. You will also find quotes that pertain directly to your desire to become a better thinker. Each puzzle in this book has been specifically chosen to help train your mind to consider different areas of thinking, some of which may be new to you. Thus, there are both mathematical teasers to test your logic/deductive reasoning powers and word puzzles, some of which have spatial/visual components, to boost your verbal skills. Even if you have to sneak a peek at some of the answers, I promise that before long you'll be amazed at how much more easily the solutions will come— and in all the different categories of puzzle types. Believe it or not, solving one type of puzzle will open gateways to solving others.

You will find that as you solve these puzzles your mind's flexibility will improve so that the more you do, the better problem solver you will become. And remember: your success in business and in life depends on your ability to solve problems.

Format

Here is the format for all sections: preceding each group of puzzles for each section is a problem-solving tip or characteristic of a great thinker. This is followed by a quote that is directly applicable to that tip or characteristic. The puzzles are then presented and were selected to feature a specific type of thinking skill for that section.

Try your best to solve each puzzle before looking at the answer. None of the puzzles requires advanced mathematics beyond first-semester algebra, nor is any specific training in any academic or professional discipline needed.

Here is a list of terms you will encounter in the following sections:

Divergent Thinking: the ability to expand the problem by viewing from different perspectives

Convergent Thinking: the ability to reduce the parameters of a problem, honing in on key factors

Spatial/Visual Thinking: the ability to think dimensionally, in some cases multidimensionally

Analytical Reasoning: For the purposes of this book, this is the ability to analyze seemingly nonconnected information and to put it into some semblance of logical order

Logical Reasoning: the ability to draw reasonable conclusions from premises. This can be done deductively, from general to specific, or inductively, from specific to general.

Part 1
Spatial/Visual Puzzles

Answers on page 21

TIP: *Keep learning and thinking in as many different areas as possible. Make it a point to read an article or on a topic you've previously had no interest in ... new connections for the mind.*

QUOTE: *"As with our muscles, we can strengthen our neural pathways with brain exercise, or we can let it wither. The principle is the same: Use it or lose it."*

Dr. John Ratey
From *A User's Guide to the Brain*

Below are some spatial/visual puzzles to solve. Remember, approach these with a sense of fun and adventure.

1. Below are five different sides of a solid object constructed out of several identical cubes fused together. What does the sixth side look like?

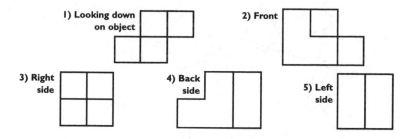

2. Which figure would best complete the following? (Think "axis.")

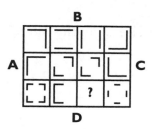

3. The square below has the four corners marked with numbered dots. Can you move two of these dots and reconnect them to the other two dots to create a new square that is exactly twice the size of the square below?

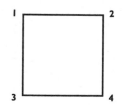

4. What is the maximum number of triangles that can be created by intersecting three triangles? Include small triangles that may be part of larger triangles.

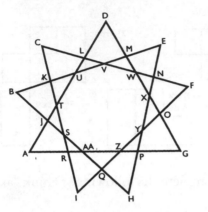

5. How many different squares of any size are in this figure?

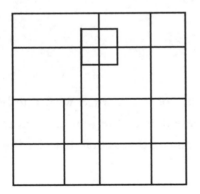

6. How creative are you? Can you solve the triangle word game below? There is a certain logic in and around the triangles that will point you to the right answer. See if you can come up with the missing letter as the lower-left corner of the third triangle.

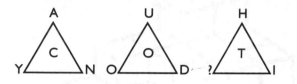

7. Below are four pieces of a puzzle that form a square when properly fitted together. Trace the four figures, cut them out and see if you can arrange them to make a square.

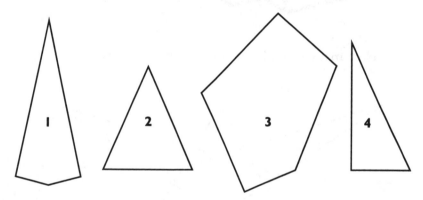

8. How many individual cubes are in this stack of cubes? Assume that all rows and columns are complete unless you actually see them end.

9. How many triangles of any size are in the figure below?

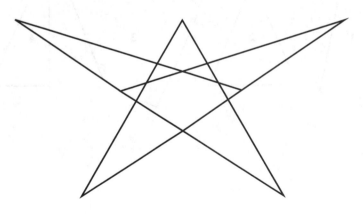

10. How many four-sided figures are in the drawing below?

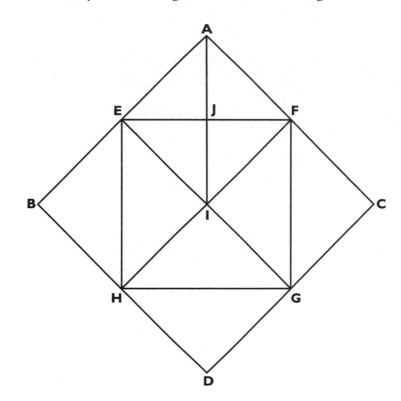

Part 1

Spatial/Visual Puzzles

A N S W E R S

1. Answer: Bottom

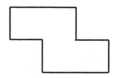

2. Answer:
Fold "A" over to "C" on the BD axis. After the folding, each of the separate boxes will have six squares of the same size. In other words, view this as a transparency where the lines map on top of each other to form six squares.

3. Answer:

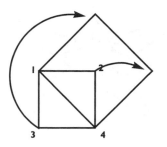

4. Answer: 30

ADG	BKS	DLW	GOZ	IRZ	MVW
A(AA)J	CFI	ENV	GPX	(AA)RS	NWX
ART	CLT	EMX	H(AA)P	JST	OXY
BEH	CKV	FOW	HQY	KTU	PYZ
BJU	DMU	FNY	IQS	LUV	QZ(AA)

5. Answer: There are only 14!

6. Answer: The answer is S. Beginning with the letter C in the middle of the first triangle, the phrase "can you do this" is spelled out.

7. Answer:

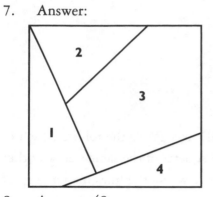

8. Answer: 49

9. Answer:

△ADL	△BIL	△EGO
△AFJ	△CEH	△EIM
△AGI	△CFO	△FGH
△AMO	△CJM	△HIJ
△BDG	△CKN	△JKL
△BEN	△CFK	△LMN
△BHK	△DNO	

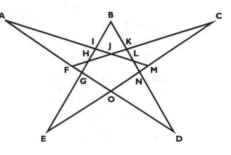

10. Answer: 24

ABCD	BEIH	DHIG
AEIF	BEGH	DHFG
ABHF	BHFE	DHEG
ACGE	BDGE	EFGH
AFHE	CGEF	EJIH
AFGE	CDHF	FJIG
AFGI	CGHF	
AIHE	CGIF	
AIGC		
AIHB		

Part 2
Frame Games

Answers on page 33

QUOTE: *"It is an old maxim of mine that when you have excluded the impossible, whatever remains, however impossible, must be the truth."*

Sherlock Holmes

Try these "Frame Game" puzzles. They will help to increase your divergent thinking, pattern recognition, spatial/visual and recall thinking skills.

Each "Frame Game" is a common phrase, name of a movie, book, song title, famous place, etc. For example:

Wear
Long

is solved to read "long underwear."

1.   Find the hidden phrase or title.

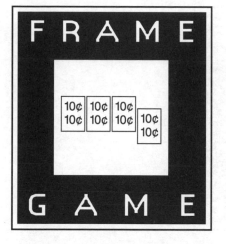

2.   Find the hidden phrase or title.

3. Find the hidden phrase or title.

4. Find the hidden phrase or title.

5. Find the hidden phrase or title.

6. Find the hidden phrase or title.

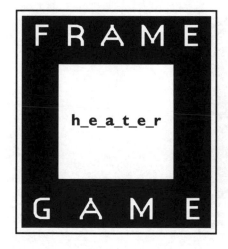

7.   Find the hidden phrase or title.

8.   Find the hidden phrase or title.

9.   Find the hidden phrase or title.

10.   Find the hidden phrase or title.

Part 2
Frame Games

A N S W E R S

1.   Answer: Paradigm shift.

2.   Answer: Double or nothing.

3.   Answer: 3 on 2 fast break.

4.   Answer: Polliwogs and tadpoles.

5.   Answer: Snooze buttons.

6.   Answer: Space heater.

7.   Answer. Poking holes in an argument.

8.   Answer: Expansion bridge.

9.   Answer: Stay on the right side of the law.

10. Answer: Mary is under the weather.

Part 3
Logical Reasoning Puzzles

Answers on page 43

Characteristic of Great Thinkers:

Great thinkers are always looking for the next mental challenge, even if it means repeated failures. They have an ability to let criticism and failures fall off their backs.

QUOTE: *"I think and think for months and years. Ninety-nine times the conclusion is false, the hundredth time I am right."*

Albert Einstein

Here are some puzzles that feature your logical reasoning and convergent thinking skills.

1. In one room of a house are three separate switches that are connected in some order to three lightbulbs in a second room. Is it possible to visit each room once and only once and determine which switches control which lights? (You may not use a screwdriver or unscrew lightbulbs to gather clues.)

2. Robert took a test of 20 questions. The test was graded by giving 10 points for each correct answer and deducting five points for each incorrect answer. Robert answered all 20 questions and received a score of 125. How many wrong answers did he have?

3. Follow the directions below and see if you can answer the two questions at the end.

    A. There are five houses; the physicist lives next to the man with the horse.
    B. The Spaniard owns a dog; there are coffee drinkers in the green house.
    C. The Belgian drinks tea; the chemist lives next to the man with the fox.
    D. The green house is immediately to the right of the white house.
    E. The mathematician owns a cat; there are milk drinkers in the middle house.
    F. The German lives in the red house; a physicist lives in the yellow house.
    G. The biologist drinks orange juice; the Norwegian lives in the first house.
    H. The Japanese is an engineer; the Norwegian lives next to the blue house.
    I. Each man has one house, a different nationality, a different pet, a different occupation, and a different choice of drinks.

    A. **Who drinks beer?**   B. **Who owns the zebra?**

4. There were 100 people present at a baseball-card show:

    59 were men
    72 were football- and baseball-card collectors
    81 were college graduates
    89 were right-handed

    What is the least number of men who were both football- and baseball-card collectors and right-handed college graduates?

5. If the four statements below are true, is the conclusion true or false?

    All good golfers own clubs that include metal woods.
    Bob owns clubs that include metal woods.
    Bob is a member of a country club.
    The last time Bob was on the country club golf course, he walked all 18 holes in the rain.

    Conclusion: Bob is a golfer.

6. You have 8 black socks and 24 blue socks in a drawer. If you reach into the drawer without looking at the socks, what is the smallest number of socks you must take from the drawer to be assured of getting one pair of black socks?

7. I saw this curious sign in a clothing store:

Men's suits:	$240	IF YOU CAN DETERMINE HOW WE ARRIVED AT
Overcoats:	$200	THE PRICE FOR EACH ITEM AND DETERMINE
Sweaters:	$200	WHAT THE PRICE OF OUR SHOES SHOULD BE,
Cufflinks:	$280	WE WILL GIVE YOU 40% OFF ON THE FIRST
Shoes	$??	FOUR ITEMS AND A PAIR OF SHOES FOR FREE.

    Could you take advantage of this opportunity?

8. This puzzle is a form of syllogism. Determine whether the conclusion reached in the last line is true or false.

> Some fids are pums
> All pums are grets
> Some grets are cips
> Therefore, some fids are definitely cips.

9. I recently returned from a trip. Today is Thursday. I returned three days before the day after the day before tomorrow. On what day did I return?

10. Is the following syllogism true or false?

> All baseball players are athletes.
> Some citizens of Omaha are athletes.
> Therefore, some citizens of Omaha are baseball players.

Part 3

Logical Reasoning
Puzzles

A N S W E R S

1.   Answer: No. This has never been proven to be possible.

2.   Answer: He had 5 wrong answers. If Robert had answered all 20
                questions correctly, he would have scored 200. Since he
                scored 125, this means he lost 75 points. We must
                deduct 15 points for each wrong answer: 10 points out
                of 200 that he *didn't* earn, plus 5 points deducted for
                the wrong answer. 75 ÷ 15 = 5 incorrect answers.

3.   Answer: The Norwegian drinks beer.
                The Japanese owns the zebra.

4.   Answer: One. If you were to add up all the four categories, the
                total is 301. This number has to be checked against the number
                of people attending the card show, which was 100. That means
                one person, at the least, fits into all four categories.

5.   Answer: False: Bob most likely is a golfer, but there is nothing
                in the statements that definitely points to a fact that Bob is a
                golfer. He may have been given the clubs and he may have been
                jogging around the golf course instead of playing golf.

6.   Answer: 26. You might just remove 24 blue socks before you pull
                out the first black sock.

7.   Answer: You could take advantage of this opportunity if you
                determined that each consonant in each of the items' names is
                worth $40, and therefore a pair of shoes would sell for $120.

8.   Answer: The conclusion is false. Some fids may be cips, but there
                is no logic to support that the conclusion is definite.

9.   Answer: The day before tomorrow is today—Thursday. The day after that is Friday. Three days before Friday is Tuesday, which is the answer.

10. Answer: While in reality there may be some baseball players in Omaha, the way this syllogism is set up makes its conclusion false because not all athletes are baseball players.

Part 4

Scrambled Quotes Puzzles

Answers on page 51

Characteristic of Great Thinkers:

It's not a coincidence that clever minds also seem to have a quick wit. It seems high level thinkers, from scientists to comedians, are able to have a little different perspective on things that result in some hilarious humor. Don't take yourself so seriously that you can't have a laugh at your own expense now and then. The legendary math and science writer, Martin Gardner, writes, "Psychologists are not sure, but studies of creative thinking suggest some sort of relationship between ability and humor."

QUOTE: *"I would never join a club that would have me as a member."*

Groucho Marx

This section has well-known, jumbled quotes—some with a humorous twist. Spatial/visual, sequential, and recall are featured thinking skills.

1. Dead three them if two of keep a secret are may.
    Benjamin Franklin

2. Interfere I my with have education let schooling never my.
    Mark Twain

3. Luck nothing people's obnoxious is as as other.
    F. Scott Fitzgerald

4. Middle difficulty in lies opportunity the of every.
    Albert Einstein

5. Further standing giants it is by upon I shoulders if seen of the have.
    Sir Isaac Newton

6. Exception forget glad to a face but I'll be I never case make your in an.
    Groucho Marx

7. Either or find make we one a way will.
    Hannibal

8. Drink nor water everywhere drop to water any.
    Samuel Taylor Coleridge

9. Watching you lot observe just can a by.
    Yogi Berra

10. Earth give which stand move place firm a me on to and I will the.
    Archimedes

Part 4

Scrambled Quotes Puzzles

A N S W E R S

1. Answer: Three may keep a secret, if two of them are dead.

2. Answer: I have never let my schooling interfere with my education.

3. Answer: Nothing is as obnoxious as other people's luck.

4. Answer: In the middle of every difficulty lies opportunity.

5. Answer: If I have seen further, it is by standing upon the shoulders of giants.

6. Answer: I never forget a face, but in your case I'll be glad to make an exception.

7. Answer: We will either find a way or make one.

8. Answer: Water, water, everywhere, nor any drop to drink.

9. Answer: You can observe a lot by just watching.

10. Answer: Give me a firm place to stand, and I will move the earth.

Part 5

Sequence Puzzles

Answers on page 59

Characteristic of Great Thinkers:

Many, if not most, great thinkers have taken their time in arriving at solutions. It seems that time was never a function of their thinking ability. In our fast-paced world, you may want to grant more leeway to those who take a little longer to arrive at a solution that affects you. It may pay big rewards.

QUOTE: *"The strongest of all warriors are these two—time and patience."*

Leo Tolstoy

Below are ten sequence puzzles where you are to fill in the missing numbers. A hint to help you: let your imagination run wild. For example, a sequence may contain numbers but not be a mathematical sequence. Anything is fair game. These are puzzles that will test your logical reasoning, pattern recognition, and divergent thinking skills.

1. 13   7   18   10   5   _?_   9   1   12   6

2. 16   21   26   26   12   5   _?_

3. −10 8   18   20   14   0   _?_

4. 2   6   12   20   30   42   _?_

5. 6   3   4   5   7   8   _?_

6. 4   2   8   5   7   _?_

7. 1Q   3E   5T   7V   _9?_

8. 3   2   6   4   9   6   12   8   15   _?_

9. 1   64   243 256 125 36   _?_

10. _?_ 19   −22 56   9   1   0   10   7

Part 5

Sequence Puzzles

A N S W E R S

1. Answer: 14. The first and last numbers added together make 19, as do the second number and next to last number. Keep moving to the middle, in pairs, from the outside in.

2. Answer: 19. The sequence actually spells out the word "puzzles." A = 1, B = 2, C = 3, etc. S = 19.

3. Answer: −22. Here is how you arrive at the solution:

   Take the differences between the numbers until you see a pattern develop . . . then you can work your way back to the answer.

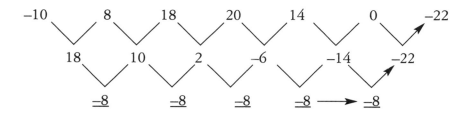

4. Answer: 56. The sequence looks like this when broken down.

$$1^2 + 1 = 2$$
$$2^2 + 2 = 6$$
$$3^2 + 3 = 12$$
$$4^2 + 4 = 20$$
$$5^2 + 5 = 30$$
$$6^2 + 6 = 42$$
$$7^2 + 7 = 56$$

5. Answer: 9. The title to Wilson Pickett's famous song "634–5789."

6. Answer: 1. This is the fraction 3/7 expressed in decimal form.

7. Answer: 0. These are the numbers and letters closest to and below the odd numbers on a standard keyboard (first row).

8. Answer: 10. There are really two different sequences working here. Starting with the first 3 and moving to every other number, you will find 3, 6, 9, 12, and 15. Do the same starting with the number 2 . . . 2, 4, 6, 8, and, therefore, 10 is the answer that follows 8.

9. Answer: 7. Here is a look at the answer that may give you a different perspective to the solution:

    $$1^7 2^6 3^5 4^4 5^3 6^2 7^1$$

10. Answer: 14. These are the correct, consecutive answers for each of the nine preceding puzzles.

Part 6
Word Power Puzzles

Answers on page 69

TIP: *Here are some ways top-notch problem solvers look at a new mental challenge: Turn the problem inside out, upside down, and sideways. Spin, twist, stretch, and break it down. Play with it (both literally and figuratively). Put the problem into different frames of reference to view it.*

QUOTE: *"Innovation comes from creative destruction."*

Yoshihisa Tabuci
CEO Normura Securities

The ways you use words say a great deal about who and what you are. Not only the words themselves, but the syntax and semantics in which they are expressed, both verbal and written, will be the main criteria people will use to form an opinion about you, especially when they first meet you.

This section has some "word power" fun. The puzzles ask for either a correct spelling or the meaning of a word. This will work your memory, concentration, and visualization abilities.

1. One of the following words is misspelled. Which one is it?

   Siege
   Vermillion
   Hagar
   Believe
   Spaghetti

2. Our English definition of the word "myriad" means a great but indefinite number. To the ancient Greeks, however, the word had a definite numerical value. What was it?

3. Below are four words—upside down so that you won't peek—that are invariably misspelled.

   Have someone read them to you and try your luck at spelling them correctly.

   Renaissance
   Commitment
   Inoculate
   Rarefy

4. Complete the following sentence:

   If you had a condition known as hyposmia, you would have a diminished sense of _____.

   Smell   Taste   Sight   Balance

5. One of the following words is misspelled. Which one?

    Queue
    Pomegranite
    Poltergeist
    Hydraulic
    Emblazon

6. What is the meaning of the word "somerset"?

7. Which word is the opposite of "probity"?

    Veracious
    Dignity
    Allegiance
    Turpitude
    Devotion

8. What is the meaning of the word "versicle"?

9. Here's a fun challenge. Below are four words—printed upside down so you won't peek—to test your spelling skill. Have someone read them to you and try your luck at spelling them correctly. (Hint: Most people stumble on the spelling of the third word.)

    Committeeman
    Commitment
    Committal
    Commit

10. Below are four familiar words that are often misspelled (printed upside down so you won't peek). If you want to test your spelling skill, stop here and have someone read the words to you.

Connoisseur

Ukulele

Puzzling

Soliloquy

11. What does the word "obstreperous" mean?

12. One of the following five words does not fit with the others. Which word is it? (Hint: It has to do with the words' meanings.)

Munificence

Magnanimity

Penury

Benevolence

Philanthropy

13. What does the word "sedulous" mean?

14. Here's a quick spelling quiz. The three words below are printed upside down so you won't peek. Have a friend read them to you and see if you can spell them correctly.

Annihilate

Reveille

Paraphernalia

15. Which of the following words is the opposite of "penurious"?

        Thrifty

        Miserly

        Exalted

        Generous

        Formidable

Part 6
Word Power Puzzles

A N S W E R S

1. Answer: "Vermilion" has only one "l."

2. "Myriad" meant 10,000.

3. Answer: Requires correct spelling of words.

4. Answer: Hyposmia is a diminished sense of smell.

5. Answer: "Pomegranate" has no *I*.

6. Answer: It means somersault.

7. Answer: "Turpitude" is the answer.

8. Answer: A versicle is a verse of sentence said or sung by a clergyman and followed by a response from the congregation.

9. Answer: (The answer is in the question.)

10. Answer: (The answer is in the question.)

11. Answer: Uncontrollably noisy.

12. Answer: "Penury," which is stinginess or miserliness, doesn't fit with the others. All the other words have to do with generosity.

13. Answer: Diligent.

14. Answer: (The answer is in the question.)

15. Answer: "Penurious" means cheap or miserly, so its opposite would be "generous."

Part 7
Analogies Puzzles

Answers on page 77

Characteristic of Great Thinkers:

When closing in on a solution, keep your emotions and personal prejudices out of it—and check your ego at the front door.

If the solution requires an emotional component, the proper weighting of that can be assigned at the end of the solution process. Work to keep an open mind.

QUOTE: *"The most characteristic feature of stupidity is not the ability to think or lack of knowledge, but the certainty with which ideas are held."*

Dr. Edward deBono

This section features analogy puzzles. These are excellent puzzles to both test and develop your ability in forming relationships, logical reasoning, sometimes spatial/visual, and finding nuances that matter in the deductive reasoning process.

1. C : 100 : : ? : 1,000,000

2. Aphrodite (Greek) : Venus (Roman) : : Poseidon (Greek) : : ? (Roman)

3. spool : top : : loops : ?

4. 100 : percentage :: 99: ?

5. 100:300 :: centenary: ?

6. heart : cardiologist :: thyroid gland : ?

7. Nebraska : Cornhusker State : : Pennsylvania : ?

8. Fox : vulpine : : wolf : ?

9. Eric Clapton : Yardbirds : : Rod Stewart : ?

10. pianissimo : very soft : : forte : ?

11. Stallion : Mare : : peacock : ?

12. Flood : deluvial : : Rain: ?

13. 5 : Lincoln : : 20 : ?

14. 3 : 27 : : 4 : ?

    (Hint: Do not consider subtraction or addition.)

15. Carbon : 6 : : Nitrogen : ?

    (Hint: It's periodic.)

Part 7

Analogies Puzzles

ANSWERS

1. Answer: $\overline{M}$ is the Roman Numeral for 1,000,000. (It must have the line over the "M" for the answer to be correct. "M," by itself, is 1000.)

2. Answer: Neptune is the Roman equivalent for the Greek god Poseidon.

3. Answer: Pot. Loops is the reverse of spool; pot is the reverse of top.

4. Answer: Percentile. 100 is the highest percentage as 99 is the highest percentile.

5. Answer: "Tercentenary" is the word to denote a 300th anniversary or celebration.

6. Answer: Endocrinologist.

7. Answer: Pennsylvania is known as the Keystone State.

8. Answer: Lupine.

9. Answer: Rod Stewart because internationally known while performing with the band Faces.

10. Answer: Loud (music).

11. Answer: Peahen. A stallion is a male and a mare, female. A peacock is a male and a peahen is female.

12. Answer: Pluvial.

13. Answer: Abraham Lincoln is on the American five-dollar bill. Andrew Jackson is on the twenty-dollar bill.

14. Answer: Either 36 or 64 is acceptable.

     a. $9 \times 3 = 27$; $9 \times 4 = 36$
     b. 3 cubed is 27; 4 cubed is 64.

15. Answer: 7. The atomic number of Carbon is 6. Likewise, the atomic number of Nitrogen is 7.

Part 8
Math Puzzles

Answers on page 87

TIP: *Make a written legend of the data, facts, and information you are given. Put it into some semblance or order that is easy for you to manipulate. The mere act of writing or typing can often trigger the mind into action.*

QUOTE: *"The best way to have consequential thoughts is to write them down."*

E. B. White

If you enjoy math brain teasers, then this section will give you a good workout. No higher math is needed. First-semester algebra will help, however. These puzzles will help to work your logical and analytical reasoning and both divergent and convergent thinking skills.

1. The Miller family has three kids. One of them, being mathematically inclined, said, "We have one boy and two girls in our family, so I bet you think the chances of a family having at least one boy is one in three, but you'd be wrong. You might be surprised if you knew what the probability is of a family with three children having at least one boy."

   What is the probability of a family with three children having at least one boy?

2. I can mow my lawn in 2 hours. My son can mow the same lawn in 2.5 hours. If we both work together, how long will it take us to mow the lawn?

3. Below is an equation where you are asked to solve for x. It is not particularly difficult, but you might be surprised to know that many people cannot solve it. The beauty of this puzzle is not so much in the answer, but in how you set up the problem to find the solution. Give it a try.

$$x^{\frac{1}{2}} + x^{\frac{1}{4}} = 20.$$

4. When you throw a pair of dice, what is the probability they will not come up 11?

5. What is the value of F?

$$
\begin{aligned}
A + B &= Z \\
Z + P &= T \\
T + A &= F \\
B + P + F &= 100 \\
A &= 8
\end{aligned}
$$

6. Which of the following expressions is the smallest in value?

    A. $\dfrac{\sqrt{10}}{10}$ B. $\dfrac{10}{\sqrt{10}}$ C. $\sqrt{10}$ D. $\dfrac{1}{\sqrt{10}}$ E. $\dfrac{1}{10\sqrt{10}}$

7. In the number square below, the numbers down and across are determined by a set of rules using arithmetic. Find the missing number in the square with the question mark.

7	10	16
13	22	40
31	58	?

8. In the square below, a certain rule applies in each of the three rows that determine each successive number. Find the rule and figure out the missing number. Remember go horizontally only.

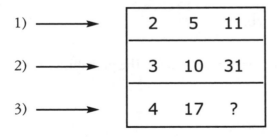

2	5	11
3	10	31
4	17	?

1) →
2) →
3) →

9. There is a number which, when added to 1⅓, will give you the same results as when it is multiplied by 1⅓. What is the number?

10. Part of a basketball team stopped by a restaurant and ordered nachos after a game. The bill came to $50, but when it came time to pay the bill, two of the team members had already left the restaurant. This meant that the remaining people had to pay an extra $1.25 to cover the bill. How many people from the team were originally at the restaurant?

11. What is the probability of three people being born on the same day? Use 365 days as a year.

12. Find the missing number in the sequence below:

    31   41   ?9   26   53   58   97

13. I am older than my sister. Fifteen years ago her age was 1/3 of what my age is now. Ten years ago my age was twice what her age was 15 years ago. What are our ages today?

14. The speed of a boat in still water is 10 mph. The boat takes a trip where it travels 45 miles upstream and 45 miles downstream. The total duration of this trip is 12 hours. Can you determine the speed of the current?

15. You need several weights of different sizes in order to be able to balance any weight from 1 to 17 pounds (in whole numbers). If you can use each weight only once for each separate weighting of 1 to 17 pounds, what is the minimum number of weights you will need? What are the weights?

Part 8

Math Puzzles

ANSWERS

1. Answer: The probability is 7 out of 8. Below is a chart showing all the possibilities involved if a family is going to have three children. In 7 of the 8 cases, it can be seen that at least one boy appears (the bold **B** represents boy).

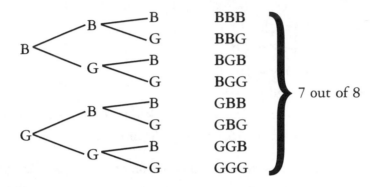

2. Answer: In 1 hour, I can mow 1/2 the lawn.

    In 1 hour, my son can mow 2/5 of the lawn.

    Together in 1 hour, we can mow 1/2 + 2/5 = 9/10 of the lawn.

    (5/10 + 4/10 = 9/10)

    So to complete the lawn mowing, it will take us 10/9 hours, or 1.111$\overline{1}$ hours.

3. Answer: x = 256 and x = 625.

    It may be helpful to restate x ½ and x ¼ into terms that are easier to handle mathematically. As an example, let x = y^4. Then you could say:

    A. y^2 + y = 20
    B. y^2 + y − 20 = 0
    C. (y + 5) (y − 4) = 0
    D. y = 4 and y = −5
    E. Plugging these 2 values back into x = y^4 would result in x = 4^4 or 256, and x = -5^4 or 625.

    Now, going back to the original equation of x ½ + x ¼ = 20, put 256 and 625, respectively, into the equation to see if it is correct.

    *A. $256^{\frac{1}{2}}$ + $256^{\frac{1}{4}}$ = 20
         16 + 4 = 20; so this is correct.
    *B. 625 ½ + 625 ¼ = 20
         25 + (-5) = 20

    *Note: there are additional roots that are not applicable to this problem.

4. Answer: 17 out of 18.

    There are only two ways 11 can be thrown: 5 and 6, and 6 and 5. This is out of 36 different possibilities (each die has 6 faces: 6 x 6 = 36). Therefore, the probability of rolling an 11 is 2/36 or 1 out of 18, which means there are 17 out of 18 chances the total will not be 11.

5. Answer: 58. Since it is known that A + B = Z, it then follows that A + B + P = T. We know that T + A = F, so in the equation B + P + F = 100, we can replace F with T + A. The equation then becomes B + P + T + A = 100 or B + P + T = 92, since A = 8. Rearranging the equations to solve for T:

$$
\begin{array}{rcl}
8 \ + \ B \ + \ P &=& T \\
\underline{92 \ - \ B \ - \ P} &=& \underline{T} \\
100 \qquad\qquad &=& 2T
\end{array}
$$

Dividing both sides by 2 gives T = 50.

Since we know that A is 8 and T + A = F, F is equal to 8 + 50, or 58.

6. Answer: E. $\dfrac{1}{10\sqrt{10}}$

7. Answer: The missing number is 112.

The rule going across is to subtract 2 from each number and multiply by 2. The rule going down is to subtract 4 from each number, multiply by 3, and add 4. So for the missing number, you can either multiply 56 × 2 = 112, going horizontally, or working down, multiply 36 × 3 = 108 and add 4 to get 112.

8. Answer: 69. The rule is to square the first number in each row and then add 1, then multiply the first two numbers in each row and add one to determine the third number.

9. Answer: 4

$$
\begin{array}{rcl}
x + 4/3 &=& 4/3\,x \\
\tfrac{3}{4}\,x + 1 &=& x \\
\tfrac{1}{4}\,x &=& 1 \\
x &=& 4
\end{array}
$$

10. Answer:

There were 10 originally. Here's one way to solve this:

Let y = the price for each player and x = the number of players

$$\frac{\$50.00}{x} = y$$
$$x \cdot y = (x - 2) \cdot (y + 1.25)$$
$$x \cdot y = x \cdot y - 2y + 1.25x - 2.50$$
$$2y = 1.25x - 2.50$$

But we know that $y = {}^{50}\!/\!_x$

$$\text{so } 2 \cdot {}^{50}\!/\!_x = 1.25x - 2.50$$
$${}^{100}\!/\!_x = 1.25x - 2.50$$
$${}^{100}\!/\!_x = \tfrac{5}{4}x - \tfrac{5}{2}$$
$${}^{400}\!/\!_x = 5x - 10$$
$$400 = 5x^2 - 10x$$
$$5x^2 - 10x - 400 = 0$$
$$x^2 - 2x - 80 = 0$$
$$(x + 8)(x - 10) = 0$$

$x = -8$ has no meaning in this problem.

$x = 10$ is the number of players originally at the restaurant.

11. Answer: One out of 133,225.

$$(\tfrac{1}{365})^3 \times 365 = \frac{1}{48,627,125} \times 365 = \frac{1}{133,225}$$

If a specific day had been given, then the chances would be $(\tfrac{1}{365})^3 \ldots$

Since it could be any of the 365 days, then the formula is $(\tfrac{1}{365})^3 \times 365$.

which is the same as $(\tfrac{1}{365})^2$.

12. Answer: 5. The sequence is really the first fourteen digits of π: 3.1415926535897.

13. Answer: I am 30; my sister is 25.

14. Answer: The speed of the current is 5 mph. Below is a table that may present a clearer picture of how to solve this.

	Distance	Speed	Time
Downstream	45 miles	10 + current	t_1
Upstream	45 miles	10 − current	t_2

Distance (d) divded by the rate (r) (speed in the table above) will give us time (t):

$$\frac{d_1}{r_1} + \frac{d_2}{r_2} = t_1 + t_2$$

And were c = current,

$$\frac{45}{10+c} + \frac{45}{10-c} = 12$$

$$45(10 - c) + 45(10 + c) = 12(100 - c^2)$$
$$450 - 46c + 450 + 45c = 1200 - 12c^2$$
$$900 = 1200 - 12c^2$$
$$0 = 300 - 12c^2$$
$$12c - 300 = 0$$
$$c^2 - 25 = 0$$
$$(c + 5)(c - 5) = 0$$

Since the speed cannot be a negative in this problem, we have:

$$c - 5 = 0$$
$$c = 5$$

The current is 5 miles per hour.

15. Answer: If you had five different weights, you could use a combination of a 9-pound weight, a 4-pound weight, a 2-pound weight, and two 1-pound weights or a combination of a 9-pound weight, a 3-pound weight, two 2-pound weights, and a 1-pound weight.

Part 9

General Knowledge/
Trivia Puzzles

Answers on page 101

TIP: *When everything fails in arriving at a solution, try one or all of the following:*

1. *Get completely away from the problem temporarily.*
2. *Talk it out with someone else (it worked for Sherlock).*
3. *Go for a long walk.*

In regard to Tip #3, there are several stories of great thinkers having that AHA! moment during a long walk (physicists Einstein and Penrose being two).

The brain seems to be able to subconsciously process information in a more relaxed manner while engaged in another activity.

As a side note, the stories of "walkers" have two interesting features to them: most of the walking was done at night and alone.

QUOTE: *"The creative process cannot be summoned at will or even cajoled by sacrificial offering. Indeed, it seems to occur most readily when the mind is relaxed and the imagination roaming freely."*

Morris Kline, *Scientific American*

General knowledge/trivia is featured in this section's puzzles. Thinking skills are memory, association, logical reasoning, and some spatial/visual.

1. Listed below are several words that are part of a larger group of something. What is that something?

   Cloche, Toque, Boater, Tricorne, Porkpie

2. If I handed you a basket full of items with names like **Baldwin, Cortland, Tydeman,** and **Idared,** what would I be giving you?

3. The branch of medicine that deals with children is called pediatrics and the branch of medicine that deals with aging is called geriatrics. What is the branch of medicine called that is concerned with obesity?

4. If you skimmed an article and saw the words *recitative, morendo, cantabile,* and *stretto,* what subject would the article address?

5. Quickly now, can you name the states that are adjacent to Nebraska?

6. The following are four successive vice presidents: Lyndon Johnson, Hubert Humphrey, Spiro Agnew, and Gerald Ford. Quickly now, who was the next in line? (10 seconds for this.)

7. What is unusual about the following sentence?

   "I am not sure every turtle paddles naturally."

8. Here's a fun analogy that will test both your history and trivia skills:

   Roy Rogers is to Trigger as Robert E. Lee is to ___?___.

9. Most of us know that a young cat is a kitten, a young dog is a puppy, and a young fox is a kit. What are the names of the young of the following animals?

     A. Kangaroo
     B. Owl
     C. Pigeon
     D. Hawk
     E. Goose

10. Below are famous people who share a specific distinction. What is it?

Gorbachev, Einstein, Hemingway, Morrison, Friedman

11. In what order should Saturn and Jupiter appear below?

Pluto, Mercury, Mars, Venus, Earth, Neptune, Uranus, ____?____, ____?____.

12. Below are five words whose letters can be reshuffled to come up with new words. Can you find a new word for each of the five in this anagram puzzle?

     A. CHATTER
     B. AMERICAN
     C. EXCLAIMS
     D. LAPSE
     E. GRAPES

13. Where would you most likely find a "spelunker"?

> In an ocean?
> In a cave?
> In a mountain?
> In a delta?

14. If you were to go "gunkholing," what would you be doing?

> Hunting?
> Fishing?
> Sailing?
> Sledding?

15. Which of the following vitamins is not water-soluble?

> Vitamin C
> Niacin
> Vitamin A
> Folic acid

Part 9

General Knowledge/ Trivia Puzzles

ANSWERS

1. Answer: These are different types of hats.

2. Answer: Apples.

3. Answer: Bariatrics (from *baros*, Greek for "weight").

4. Answer: Music. These terms would most likely be found in classical music such as opera or chamber music.

5. Answer: Beginning with South Dakota, which is north of Nebraska, and continuing clockwise, the states are Iowa, Missouri, Kansas, Colorado, and Wyoming.

6. Answer: Nelson Rockefeller.

7. Answer: Each word has one more letter than the word before it.

8. Answer: Traveller was the name of General Lee's horse.

9. Answer:

      A. Kangaroo — Joey
      B. Owl — Owlet
      C. Pigeon — Squab
      D. Hawk — Eyas
      E. Goose — Gosling

10. Answer: All are Nobel Prize winners.

11. Answer: Saturn, then Jupiter. The planets are listed by increasing diameter.

12. Answer

      A. CHATTER — RATCHET
      B. AMERICAN — CINERAMA
      C. EXCLAIMS — CLIMAXES
      D. LAPSE — PALES OR SEPAL
      E. GRAPES — PAGERS

13. Answer: In a cave. A spelunker is a cave explorer.

14. Answer: You would be sailing.

15. Answer: Vitamin A is not water-soluble.

Part 10

Geography, Geology, and Astronomy Puzzles

Answers on page 111

Geography, Geology
and Astronomy
Puzzles

TIP: *Unless you are a columnist or television commentator, leave cynicism alone. However, healthy, respectful skepticism is a must for growth and success. In business, if a proposition is not well grounded and supported by logic and evidence, be skeptical . . . and be ready to back it up.*

QUOTE: *"In order to seek truth, it is necessary once in a course of our life to doubt as far as possible all things."*

René Descartes

How well do you know geography, geology, and astronomy? Some people are amazing in their ability to understand their surroundings and how everything fits together. Try your skill with the following puzzles that will give your mind a good workout. These puzzles offer a good cross section of thinking skills from general knowledge to deductive reasoning.

1. Four of the five words below are different types of winds found around the world. Which one doesn't belong?

   A. Sirocco
   B. Chinook
   C. Mistral
   D. Levanter
   E. Corona

2. In 13,000 years, the Northern Hemisphere will have summer in December, January, and February. In another 13,000 years, it will return to what it is now. This 26,000-year cycle is called _____ ?

3. A solar day is 24 hours. There is another measurement of a day based on the length of time it takes the star pattern to return to the same position in the sky. The length of this day is 23 hours, 56 minutes, and 4.09 seconds. What is the name of this day?

4. A resident of Nebraska is referred to as a Nebraskan. If you are from Florida, you are a Floridian, and from California, a Californian. What are residents of Vermont called?

5. One of the following cities does not belong with the other four. Based on a geographical reason, which is the odd one out?

   Boston, Buffalo, Chicago, Cleveland, Milwaukee

6. What do the following terms describe?

> Miller cylindrical
> Mollweide homolographic
> Sinusoidal
> Robinson
> Conic

7. Fill in this geographical analogy:

> *East* is to *West* as *Orient* is to _____?_____.

8. How is your knowledge of nicknames of states? Here are five states. List their nicknames.

> Iowa
> Georgia
> Washington
> Pennsylvania
> Arizona

9. What are the nicknames of the following US cities?

> Denver
> New Orleans
> Houston
> Boston
> Detroit

10. In geography, there is a specific definition used to identify a *sound*. What is a *sound*?

11. The following are five of the ten different types of clouds. What are the remaining five?

> Cumulus, stratus, cirrus, cumulonimbus, stratocumulus

12. Which of the following words is the odd one out, and why?

> Continent, island, strait, isthmus, peninsula

13. What people are adjacent to Russia, Norway, and Sweden?

14. If a strait is a narrow channel joining two larger bodies of water, what is a narrow strip of land connecting two larger land masses?

15. Complete the following analogy:

> Myanmar : Burma : : Thailand : _____?_____.

Part 10

Geography, Geology, and Astronomy Puzzles

A N S W E R S

1. Answer: E. Corona.

2. Answer: Precession.

3. Answer: A sidereal day.

4. Answer: Vermonters.

5. Answer: Boston is the only city not located on a Great Lake.

6. Answer: They are different types of maps.

7. Answer: Occident.

8. Answer:

> Iowa: The Hawkeye State
> Georgia: The Empire State of the South
> Washington: The Evergreen State
> Pennsylvania: The Keystone State
> Arizona: The Grand Canyon State

9. Answer:

> Denver: The Mile-High City
> New Orleans: The Crescent City
> Houston: The Bayou City
> Boston: America's Walking City (also called "Hub of
> the Universe" and "Beantown")
> Detroit: The Motor City (also called "Motown")

10. Answer: A *sound* is a body of water separating an island from the mainland or a wide channel linking two large bodies of water. For instance, Long Island Sound separates Long Island from the mainland of New York and Connecticut.

11. Answer: Altocumulus, altostratus, cirrostratus, nimbostratus, cirrocumulus.

12. Answer: Strait. All the rest are land masses. (A strait is a waterway connecting two large bodies of water.)

13. Answer: The Finnish.

14. Answer: An isthmus.

15. Myanmar was once known as Burma; Thailand was once called Siam.

Part 11
Trickledown Puzzles

Answers on page 121

Characteristic of Great Thinkers:

One of the most interesting features of good thinkers is they are never content in just solving the current problem at hand. They mentally keep creating new problems and are constantly asking the question "what if"? They have an insatiable desire to always go to the next level.

QUOTE: *"Opportunity does not come to those who wait. It is captured by those who attack."*

Gen. Douglas McArthur

One of the best ways to make new brain connections is not only to solve puzzles and other mental challenges, but also to create your own. I can assure you it will put your mind on a whole different plane. Now is your chance. Below are puzzles called Trickledowns. The object to solve them is to change one letter on each line to make a new word. Do this to arrive at the final word of the puzzle.

Example: One way to solve this is as follows:

Game   Game

_____   Same

_____   Sane

_____   Sang

Song   Song

These puzzles can be lots of fun because they are not particularly difficult and can be solved fairly quickly. They can also have more than one word on each of the lines that is acceptable in solving the puzzle.

Your job: After solving the 10 puzzles you see here, create 10 of your own. Try to include 4-, 5-, and 6-letter Trickledowns. You might also discover you have the ability to be a puzzle creator!

1. List

    ‾‾‾‾
    ‾‾‾‾
    ‾‾‾‾
    Maps

2. Fact

    ‾‾‾‾
    ‾‾‾‾
    ‾‾‾‾
    Pure

3. Gloom

    ‾‾‾‾
    ‾‾‾‾
    ‾‾‾‾
    ‾‾‾‾
    Bread

4. Fold

    ‾‾‾‾
    ‾‾‾‾
    ‾‾‾‾
    Bare

5. Stare

    ‾‾‾‾
    ‾‾‾‾
    ‾‾‾‾
    ‾‾‾‾
    Phony

6. Wisp

———

———

———

Rope

7. Tailor

———

———

———

———

———

Footed

8. Lame

———

———

———

Sort

9. Tricky

———

———

———

———

Clangs

10. Crest

____

____

____

____

Shows

Part 11
Trickledown Puzzles

A N S W E R S

1. Answer: Note: you may have different words than my answers. As long as you arrive at the solution, your answers are correct as well.

> List
> Mist
> Miss
> Mass
> Maps

2. Answer: Fact
> Pact
> Pace
> Pare
> Pure

3. Answer: Gloom
> Bloom
> Broom
> Brood
> Broad
> Bread

4. Answer: Fold
> Bold
> Bald
> Bale
> Bare

5. Answer: Stare
                Share
                Shore
                Shone
                Phone
                Phony

6. Answer: Wisp
                Wise
                Rise
                Rose
                Rope

7. Answer: Tailor
                Tailer
                Tailed
                Failed
                Foiled
                Fooled
                Footed

8. Answer: Lame
                Same
                Some
                Sore
                Sort

9.   Answer: Tricky
                   Tricks
                   Tracks
                   Cracks
                   Cranks
                   Clanks
                   Clangs

10. Answer: Crest
                   Chest
                   Chess
                   Chews
                   Chows
                   Shows

Part 12
Phrizzled Phrases Puzzles

Answers on page 131

TIP: *Don't let technology be a roadblock in your thinking pursuits. Strength and flexibility are ultimately your best tools. Remember that Einstein's "technology" was pencil on paper.*

QUOTE: *"You already possess everything necessary to become great."*

Crow Indian Proverb

The next group of puzzles is called "Phrizzled phrases." Each puzzle is a sentence containing initial letters of significant words. They also contain one number that is your hint as to what the phrase will spell. These puzzles will flex your recall, logic, and general knowledge abilities.

Example: There are 100 Y on a FF.

Answer: There are 100 yards on a football field (unless you play football in Canada where the field is 110 yards).

1. There are 13 C in a S of PC.

2. There are 206 B in the HB.

3. There are 106 E in the PT.

4. There are 5 and sometimes 6 V in the A.

5. There are 5 R in the OF.

6. There are 10 T on a S. (Hint: ocean)

7. There are 13 D in a BD.

8. There are 8 N in an O.

9. There are 10 Y in a D.

10. There are 1760 Y in a M.

Part 12

Phrizzled Phrases
Puzzles

A N S W E R S

1.   Answer: There are 13 cards in a suit of playing cards.

2.   Answer: There are 206 bones in the human body.

3.   Answer: There are 106 elements in the periodic table.

4.   Answer: There are 5 and sometimes 6 vowels in the alphabet.

5.   Answer: There are 5 rings in the Olympic Flag.

6.   Answer: There are 10 tentacles on a squid.

7.   Answer: There are 13 donuts in a baker's dozen.

8.   Answer: There are 8 notes in an octave.

9.   Answer: There are 10 years in a decade.

10. Answer: There are 1760 yards in a mile.

Part 13

Verbal Sequence Puzzles

Answers on page 139

Verbal Sequence
Puzzles

TIP: *After you've reached a solution, always plug your answer back into the problem to see if it fits all the parameters you were asked to consider. Then put different solutions back into the problem . . . for checks and balances. You may find more than one answer.*

If you are having difficulty arriving at any solution, try a cross section of arbitrary solutions. That may help to narrow the range of possibilities.

QUOTE: *"The most erroneous stories are those we think we know best— and therefore never scrutinize or question."*

Stephen Jay Gould

Try a different twist on sequence puzzles . . . all verbal. General knowledge, memory, and logic are featured.

Note: It's okay to use any reference material to solve these puzzles.

1. Cervical, thoracic, lumbar, sacra, _____?_____.

2. Squad, platoon, company, battalion, brigade, _____?_____.

3. Tetrahedron, cube, octahedron, dodecahedron, _____?_____.

4. Thousand, million, billion, trillion, quadrillion, _____?_____.

5. Washington, Adams, Jefferson, Madison, Monroe, _____?_____.

6. Sea level, _____?_____, stratosphere, mesosphere, thermosphere, exosphere.

7. Groucho, Harpo, Cheeko, Zeppo, _____?_____.

8. Preposition, noun, pronoun, adjective, adverb, _____?_____, _____?_____, _____?_____.

9. Uni -, Bi - , Tri - , Quad - , Quint - , Sex - , _____?_____.

10. Susan Sarandon, Frances McDormand, Helen Hunt, Gwyneth Paltrow, Hilary Swank, _____?_____.

Part 13

Verbal Sequence Puzzles

A N S W E R S

1. Answer: Coccygeal. These are the names of the human vertebrae, moving from the head down.

2. Answer: Division. This is a hierarchy of military units beginning with the smallest.

3. Answer: Icosahedron. These are the 5 Platonic solids.

4. Answer: Quintillion (18 zeros).

5. Answer: John Quincy Adams. The first six presidents.

6. Answer: Troposphere. These are the consecutive atmospheric layers.

7. Answer: Gummo was the fifth Marx brother.

8. Answer: In any order: conjunction, interjection, and verb. These are the 8 parts of speech.

9. Answer: Any form of Sept- is acceptable. These are the Latin prefixes denoting 1 through 7.

10. Julia Roberts. These are the last 6 consecutive winners of the Academy Award for "Best Actress" (through 2000).

Part 14
Anagrams

Answers on page 147

Characteristic of Great Thinkers:

Great thinkers prefer to do their most serious thinking alone. This may seem at odds in the business world where committees, boards, and teams are prevalent and encouraged. The smart corporation realizes there is a way to accommodate both situations with great advantage to their strategic initiatives.

QUOTE: *"My idea of a board meeting is when I see my face in the mirror when I shave."*

Warren Buffett

One of the best puzzles to stretch your mental flexibility is anagrams. Anagrams are words that contain letters that will create a brand new word. Example: <u>GRAPES</u> can be changed to <u>PAGERS</u>. If you spend a little time each day trying to change words into anagrams, you will be amazed at how quickly your skill improves. Just as important: you are making new connections in the brain. These puzzles are an excellent example of divergent thinking skills, recall, and spatial/visual skills. The reason for spatial/visual? Certain combination of letters are not seen in English and your mind will immediately discard those possibilities.

1. Joe drank too much coffee, became w __ __ __ d and started acting w __ __ __ d.

2. It didn't take the Board of Directors long to come to the r __ __ __ __ __ __ __ __ __ __ n that if they had to r __ __ __ __ __ __ __ __ __ e their decisions, they weren't well thought out.

3. Even though her reports were considered to be well done, Melanie c __ __ __ __ __ __ __ d to go u __ __ __ __ __ __ __ __ d.

4. P __ __ __ __ o! Even though the artist had virtually no time, he was able to create a beautiful p __ __ __ __ r for the exhibit.

5. After spending most of her free time with this book, Maria's friend said, "I guess she just l __ __ __ s to s __ __ __ e puzzles!"

6. Because the cadet made such a favorable i __ __ __ __ __ __ __ __ __ n, he was given p __ __ __ __ __ __ __ __ n for a weekend leave.

7. How many different anagrams can you create from the word "integral"?

8. How many different anagrams can you create from the world "allergy"?

9. 4 of the 5 words below have anagrams. Can you come up with the anagrams and the odd one out?

    A. Course
    B. Blessing
    C. Cranium
    D. Various
    E. Prettiness

10. Try to come up with an anagram phrase for a well-known person. Examples:

    George Bush — He bugs Gore
    Bill Gates — Bag it — Sell!
    David Letterman — In mad, altered TV.

It is even more fun if you can make the phrase directly applicable to the person.

Part 14

Anagrams

A N S W E R S

1. Answer: wired, weird.

2. Answer: realization, rationalize.

3. Answer: continued, unnoticed.

4. Answer: presto, poster.

5. Answer: loves, solve.

6. Answer: impression, permission.

7. Answer: triangle, relating, altering, alerting.

8. Answer: largely, regally, gallery.

9. Answer:

>   A. Course — Source
>   B. Blessing — Glibness
>   C. There are no anagrams for cranium
>   D. Various — Saviour
>   E. Prettiness — Persistent

Part 15
Potpourri

Answers on page 157

Characteristic of Great Thinkers:

Great minds are often seen as unreasonable people. Sometimes they have thought out a situation through more levels than their associates, causing those around these thinkers to draw wrong conclusions about them and their solutions. So be it. Keep thinking and forging ahead of the pack!

QUOTE: *"The reasonable man adapts himself to the world. The unreasonable man persists in trying to adapt the world to himself. Therefore, all progress depends on the unreasonable man."*

George Bernard Shaw

This section contains twenty puzzles, most of which have not been included in any previous section. They cover the range of thinking skills but all require you to view them other than "head on." In other words, think "outside the box," but keep the disciplines of evidence and logic in reaching their solutions. The best way to do this is to have fun with them!

1. There's something wrong with the following sentence; give yourself about 30 seconds to discover what it is.

    Wilt Chamberlain was one of the most
    prolific scorers in the history of the
    the National Basketball Association.

2. Below is a list of famous Latin phrases. Can you come up with their English translation?

    A. Carpe diem
    B. Caveat emptor
    C. Mea culpa
    D. Cave canem
    E. Tempus fugit
    F. E pluribus unum
    G. Semper fidelis
    H. "Veni, vidi, vici"

3. The following capital letters share a common characteristic that the other capital letters in the alphabet don't have. What is it? (HINT: Think in terms of how these letters are constructed.)

    F G J L N P Q R S Z

4. What nine-letter word is written in the square below? You may start at any letter and go either clockwise or counterclockwise. The circled E is the last letter of the word.

    S   C   L
    I (E) O
    W   K   C

5. If Alex's son is my son's father, what am I to Alex?

        A. His grandfather.
        B. His father.
        C. His son.
        D. His grandson.
        E. I am Alex.

6. I recently returned from a trip. Today is Thursday. I returned three days before the day after the day before tomorrow. On what day did I return?

7. In what hobby would you find the following symbols?

    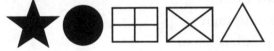

8. With one straight line, turn the following three numbers into 445:

        15   10   5

9. The following five words are related. How?

        Gilt   Shoat   Chuffy   Barrow   Wiener

10. Most of us know that a group of lions is called a *pride* of lions and that a group of sheep is called a *flock* of sheep. See if you can come up with the proper collective name for the following animals:

        turtles   crows   leopards   bees   pigs

11. In what sport would you find the following terms?

        Dormie (or dormy), fade, stymie, double-cross

12. The six words you see here share an interesting trait. Can you find out what it is?

Crude   seal   tear   general   pool   swipe

Hint: Two, at least, for the price of one.

13. The following is in code. Can you crack the code and decipher the message?

WOBBI MRBSCDWKC!

14. How many numbers are in the following series if all terms are including?

0, 3, 6, 9, 12, 15, 18, ..., 960

15. The six words listed here share a common trait:

pride   slime   grant   price   globe   whole

What is it?

16. Which one of the following vegetables doesn't belong with the others? Why?

Radishes
Peas
Carrots
Potatoes
Onions

17. Here's an odd puzzle even though you may not agree. Where should the numbers 9 and 10 be placed, above or below the line?

$$\frac{1 \quad 2 \quad 3 \qquad\qquad 6 \quad 7 \quad 8}{0 \qquad\qquad\quad 4 \quad 5}$$

18. Below are five words that can become five different words when the same three letters are added to the beginning of each word. Which three-letter combination will do the trick?

> MATE
> LET
> PATE
> ACE
> TRY

19. How can you make 100 using three nines and a zero? You can use any combination of math signs or operations.

20. When that "light" goes on, and you see clearly, for the first time, the answer you've been seeking, it's like magic. Mathematically, that moment is expressed:

> **AH!**
> **HA!**
> **A B R A** (CADABRA)

Can you come up with the correct mathematical operation and the digits to replace the letters, knowing that zero cannot begin a word, and that neither the exclamation points nor the word "CADABRA" are part of the puzzle?

Part 15
Potpourri

A N S W E R S

1. Answer: The word "the" is repeated. It appears at the end of the first line and again at the beginning of the second line.

2. Answer:

> A. Seize the day
> B. Let the buyer beware
> C. My fault
> D. Beware of the dog
> E. Time flies
> F. One out of many
> G. Always faithful
> H. "I came, I saw, I conquered" (Caesar)

3. Answer: They have no symmetry about either their vertical axis or their horizontal axis.

4. Answer: The word is "clockwise."

5. Answer: C. His son.

6. Answer: The day before tomorrow is today—Thursday. The day after that is Friday. Three days before Friday is Tuesday, which is the answer.

7. Answer: All those symbols are found in stamp collecting.

8. Answer: Add the straight line to the top of the "1" in "10": 15 TO 5. On a clock face, fifteen to five is 4:45!

9. Answer: All of them relate to pigs.

10. Answer: A bale of turtles; a murder of crows; a leap of leopards; a swarm of bees; a litter of pigs.

11. Answer: Golf.

12. Answer: All of the words have at least two very different meanings.

13. Answer: MERRY CHRISTMAS! To decode, find the code letter in the bottom row and translate it into the corresponding letter in the top row.

    Q R S T U V W X Y Z A B C D E F G H I J K L M N O P
    A B C D E F G H I J K L M N O P Q R S T U V W X Y Z

14. Answer: 321. Divide 3 into 960 and add 1.

15. Answer: Each is a 5-letter word that becomes a 4-letter word when its first letter is removed.

16. Answer: Peas. All the other vegetables are grown underground.

17. Answer: 9 goes below the line, 10 above. The hint was in the question, referring to even and odd: the numbers above the line have an odd number of letters in the spelling of their names; below the line, the names have an even number of letters.

18. Answer: PAL.

    PALMATE
    PALLET
    PALPATE
    PALACE
    PALTRY

19. Answer: Here's one way: $99 + 9° = 99 + 1$, or 100.

20. Answer:

$$
\begin{array}{rr}
\text{AH!} & 59 \\
\underline{\text{HA!}} \; = & \underline{\times 95} \\
\text{A B R A} & 5605
\end{array}
$$